It's All

MW00943554

Table of Contents

by Barbara A. Donovan

Getting Started

Look around your classroom. What things do you see? You might say "a clock," "a desk," or "a window." Everything you named is made up of **matter**.

Matter is everywhere. The books you read, the air you breathe, and the water you drink are all made up of matter.

Water is matter. In this picture, it's the **liquid** that the fish swims in. Water is a **solid** when it's ice or snow. It's a **gas** in the air. Liquids, solids, and gases are different kinds of matter.

3

Solid, Liquid, or Gas?

Solids have shapes that you can touch and feel. They might be hard like a bike or soft like a feather. They might be big like a truck or small like a bean. Each solid has a shape of its own.

The water in this puddle is a liquid. A liquid is matter that flows. A liquid gets its shape from whatever container it is in. The liquid could be in a jar, a glass, or a pool.

If we could peek inside these balloons, what would we see? Nothing! Why? These balloons are filled with a gas. We can't see or feel most gases. A gas fills the space it is in and takes the same shape.

Heat It!

Let's say the sun is shining on trees that are covered with ice. What happens? The ice starts to melt. Why? When we add enough heat to a solid, it changes the solid to a liquid. It takes a lot of heat to melt solids like gold or steel. It doesn't take as much heat to melt ice.

The water from melting ice makes puddles. When the hot sun shines on the puddles, they dry up. Heating a liquid can make it turn into a gas. Water that is a gas is called **water vapor**.

We often change matter when we cook food. Butter changes from a solid to a liquid when we melt it in a pan. Some of the water in soup changes to gas when we heat it.

Chill It!

Here's a puzzle. We use heat to turn a solid into a liquid. How can we change a liquid back into a solid? Chill it!

If we freeze water, we get ice. When we freeze liquid matter, we make it solid.

If we chill water vapor, it will change into a liquid. That's why drops of water form on a cold glass. When water vapor in the air touches the glass, the water vapor cools and turns back into a liquid. Then the drops of water slide down the glass.

When water vapor in the air cools, it can form clouds. As the gas cools, it changes into rain. Rain fills puddles, streams, and seas. On a sunny day, the water turns back into water vapor and forms clouds. This is called the **water cycle**.

Mix It!

At the beach, what might we see in the sand? Rocks and seashells? A lost penny or key? Other solids might also be mixed in the sand.

Sometimes when solids are mixed together, we can pick out each one. If we just want the seashells, we can pick them out of the sand.

Suppose we dig up clams. It would be muddy work! Mud is part solid and part liquid. The bits of dirt or sand are solids. The water is liquid. It is hard to separate the solids from the liquid in mud.

Matter is everywhere around you. You can look for solids and liquids wherever you go. Gases are all around you, too. What kinds of matter might you find at home, at the beach, or at school?

Index